DATE DUE			
GAYLORD			PRINTED IN U.S.A.

HISTORY IN ART

ANCIENT ROME

Raintree
Chicago, Illinois

PETER CHRISP

© 2005 Raintree
Published by Raintree, a division of Reed Elsevier, Inc.
Chicago, Illinois
Customer Service 888-363-4266
Visit our website at www.raintreelibrary.com

For information, address the publisher:
Raintree, 100 N. LaSalle, Suite 1200, Chicago, IL 60602

Originated by Dot Gradations Ltd.
Printed and bound in China
by South China Printing Company.

09 08 07 06
10 9 8 7 6 5 4 3 2

Library of Congress Cataloging-in-Publication Data

Chrisp, Peter.
  Ancient Rome / Peter Chrisp.
    p. cm. -- (History in art)
  Includes index.
  ISBN 1-4109-0520-9
  1. Art, Roman--Juvenile literature. 2. Rome--Civilization--Juvenile literature. I. Title. II. Series.
  N5760.C547 2005
  709'.37--dc22
                                    2004007567

Acknowledgments

The publishers would like to thank the following for permission to reproduce photographs (t = top, b = bottom): Academia Italia, London p. **31**; AKG-images/Pirozzi p. **39**; The Art Archive/Dagli Orti pp. **3** (Archaeological Museum Florence), **6** (Museo Capitolino Rome), **7**(b) (Museo della Civilta Romana Rome), **8**(b), **11** (Archaeological Museum Florence), **13**(t), **14**(t) (Archaeological Museum Venice), **14**(b) (Acropolis Museum Athens), **15** (Jan Vinchon Numismatist Paris), **16** (Museo della Civilta Romana Rome), **17**(t), **18**(b) (Musee des Beaux Arts Besancon), **22** (Museo Capitolino Rome), **24** (Archaeological Museum Madrid), **25**(b) (Museo della Civilta Romana Rome), **26** (Museo della Civilta Romana Rome), **28** (Museo Capitolino Rome), **29**, **30** (House of the poet Menander Pompeii), **32** (Archaeological Museum Naples), **33** (Archaeological Museum Naples), **35** (Musee du Louvre Paris), **36** (Museo Capitolino Rome), **37**(t) (Antiquarium Castellamare di Stabia Italy), **37**(b) (Museo della Civilta Romana Rome), **38** (Museo Nazionale Romano Rome), **40** (Archaeological Museum Naples), **41**(t) (Archaeological Museum Venice), **41**(b) (San Clemente Basilica Rome), **42**, **43** (San Vitale Ravenna Italy), **45**; Bridgeman Art Library pp. **1**, **5**(t), **8**(t), **9**, **10** (Index), **12**, **17**(b), **18**(t), **19** (Ken Welsh), **23**, **25**(t), **27**, **34**; Corbis pp. **4** (©Wolfgang Kaehler), **5**(b) (©Richard Klune), **7**(t) (©Alinari Archives), **21**(t) (Werner Forman); Getty Images/PhotoDisc pp. **20**, **21**(b), **44**.

Cover photograph of a marble bust of the Roman Emperor Augustus, reproduced with permission of the Art Archive.

Every effort has been made to contact copyright holders of any material reproduced in this book. Any omissions will be rectified in subsequent printings if notice is given to the publishers.

The paper used to print this book comes from sustainable resources.

Contents

The Roman Empire

Art provides us with a rich source of information about life in the past. No ancient civilization has left us more art, spread over a wider area, than that of Rome. At its height, in the 100 years C.E., the Roman **Empire** included all the lands around the Mediterranean Sea, stretching from Britain in the north to North Africa in the south, and from Spain in the west to Iraq in the east. This vast area included a population of around a hundred million people.

Romanization

The Romans encouraged the many different peoples within the empire to follow a similar way of life—to worship Roman gods, wear Roman clothes, and speak the Latin language. Across the empire, people used the same coins and ate from the same types of tableware. Art and architecture were also used to create a uniform Roman identity. If you traveled to any Roman town, you would see similar statues and temples. The homes of the rich would be decorated with the same types of wall paintings, following fashions set in Rome.

▼ The Arc de Triomphe du Carrousel in Paris is a copy of a Roman arch. It was built in 1805–1806 by the French emperor, Napoleon Bonaparte, to commemorate his armies' victories.

Napoleon rides a chariot, like a victorious Roman general.

Napoleon originally took ancient Roman bronze horses from Venice to pull this chariot, but these have since been returned and replaced with replicas.

Statues of French soldiers

Fine sandstone, brought all the way from Italy

Victoria, winged Roman goddess of victory

Columns made of red marble from southern France

A triumphal arch was both a monument and a ceremonial entrance, used for victory processions.

Napoleon's arch is a copy of a Roman arch, built in 203 C.E. by Emperor Septimius Severus.

The legacy of Rome

We are still influenced in countless ways by the ancient Romans. We use the Roman alphabet and follow a calendar with months named after Roman gods and rulers. March, for example, is named after the war god Mars. Our coins, with portraits of rulers in profile, surrounded by Latin words, are similar to Roman coins. Many of our customs, including birthday parties and major festivals, are Roman in origin. All over Europe, people still live in cities, such as Paris and London, originally built by the Romans.

From the late 1700s, architects in Europe and the United States imitated **Classical** architecture. Many public buildings, such as libraries and town halls, were based on Roman temples, with rows of columns (a style that the Romans themselves copied from the Greeks). In the 1800s, when European nations conquered their own empires, they copied Roman victory monuments, setting up triumphal arches, such as the Arc de Triomphe in Paris and Marble Arch in London. Bronze statues of kings, queens, and generals on horseback are also Classical in origin.

▼ Birmingham, England's town hall, built in 1832–49, is based on three surviving columns of a ruined Roman temple, dedicated to Castor and Pollux.

▼ In 1447–50, the Italian artist Donatello made this huge bronze equestrian statue, the first large-scale bronze work to be made since Roman times. He was inspired by the statue of Emperor Marcus Aurelius (see page 6).

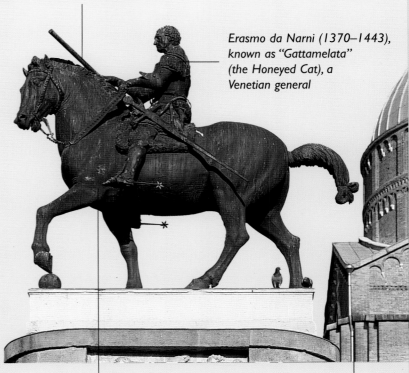

He holds a baton of command in his raised right hand.

Erasmo da Narni (1370–1443), known as "Gattamelata" (the Honeyed Cat), a Venetian general

The horse is a copy of Roman bronze horses in Venice.

The cathedral of Padua

Winning hearts and minds

The historian Tacitus described how his father-in-law, Agricola, governor of Britain, turned the recently conquered Britons into Romans:

"Agricola gave private encouragement and official assistance to the building of temples, public squares, and good houses ... Furthermore, he trained the sons of the chiefs in the liberal arts ... The result was that in place of loathing the Latin language they became eager to speak it effectively. In the same way, our national dress came into favor and the toga was everywhere to be seen."

Looking at Roman Art

We can learn a lot about the Romans from their art. Sculpture and paintings, for example, show us details of dress and hairstyles. We will learn even more if we try to discover why a piece of art was made, and how it would have been seen by an ancient Roman.

Emperor on horseback

In Rome today, you can see an 11.5-foot (3.5-meter) bronze statue of the emperor Marcus Aurelius riding a horse. When new, it was covered in gold leaf, though only faint traces now remain. Glittering in the Sun, it must have been a spectacular sight.

Clues

To understand what this statue meant to its original viewers, we have to look for clues, like a detective. One clue is the emperor's long cloak, called a *paludamentum*. This was worn only in wartime by army commanders. Another clue comes from a guidebook to Rome published in the 1100s. It records that the work once included another figure: a **barbarian**, or foreign enemy of Rome. He lay beneath the horse's raised hoof, begging for his life. The figure, now missing, explains why the emperor has his right arm outstretched with his hand open. This gesture, often made by emperors in Roman art, meant the offering of mercy to a defeated enemy. So the statue was supposed to show that Marcus Aurelius was both a victorious general and a merciful ruler.

▼ This statue of Marcus Aurelius is thought to have been made soon after his death in 180 C.E., when he was declared to have become a god.

The rider was identified as Marcus Aurelius thanks to his coin portraits; they show the same long face with curly hair and beard.

Arm outstretched, showing mercy to the defeated

The paludamentum (military cloak) shows us that the emperor is a general.

Traces of gold leaf

Veins stand out on the legs.

The statue shows us what Roman saddles looked like, with layers of leather cut to give decorative edges.

The emperor has no stirrups, for these had not yet been invented.

A fallen figure once lay here.

How did it survive?

Bronze equestrian (horse-and-rider) statues of emperors were common sights in every Roman city. Yet the statue of Marcus Aurelius is the only complete example to survive. The rest were all melted down for their valuable metal. The reason this one survived is that the pope, who kept the statue in his palace garden, wrongly thought it was of the first Christian emperor, Constantine, so it was protected by the Church.

Trajan's column

A wonderful source for evidence about the Roman army is a 125-foot (38-meter) stone column, set up in Rome by the emperor Trajan. This is covered with carvings showing Trajan's troops on campaign. Thanks to these carvings, we can see how Roman soldiers marched, built camps, crossed rivers, and fought battles. Yet the main purpose of the column was not to record military information, but to celebrate Emperor Trajan, whose statue originally stood on top and who appears in many of the scenes, giving orders and encouraging his men. After his death, Trajan's ashes were placed in the base of the column, now his tomb.

Both Marcus Aurelius's statue and Trajan's column were made to impress the people of Rome with their ruler. Today we call such work **propaganda**—art intended to push a political message across.

The original statue of Trajan was removed in the Middle Ages. This statue, of St. Peter, was placed on top in 1587 by Pope Sixtus V.

◀ Trajan's column is decorated with a long spiral frieze, with **reliefs** showing two wars that the emperor fought in Dacia (modern Romania).

The shaft is made of nineteen drums of Italian marble, each weighing around 35.2 tons (32 metric tons).

◀ This scene from Trajan's column shows the army traveling along a river in warships known as biremes, so-called because of their two rows of oars, one above the other (*bi* means two).

The Story of Rome

One of the oldest surviving works of Roman art, dating from around 500 B.C.E., is a bronze she-wolf. The she-wolf also appeared on Roman coins, and plays a key role in a legend about Rome's beginnings. According to this legend, the city's founder and first king, Romulus, had been abandoned as a baby along with his twin brother, Remus, and had been suckled by a wolf.

The twins were sons of the war god Mars. The historian Livy wrote, "If any nation deserves the privilege of claiming a **divine** ancestry, it is our own. The glory won by the Roman people in their wars is so great that, when they declare that Mars himself was their first parent, all nations of the world should accept their claim." In fact, **archaeology** shows that Rome had much humbler beginnings. In the 900 or 800 years B.C.E., It started as a scattered group of villages that slowly grew into a town.

▼ The bronze she-wolf stood on Rome's Capitoline Hill, the most sacred part of the city.

The she-wolf is shown in a protective attitude, looking around her with her ears pricked up.

Her ribs stand out, showing that she has gone hungry in order to stay with the babies.

The figures of Romulus and Remus were added in the 1400s.

Greek influence

In southern Italy, there were cities founded by the Greeks, such as Paestum and Naples. The Greeks influenced both the Etruscans and the Romans, who imitated their architecture and sculpture. The Romans copied the three orders (styles) of Greek temples, known as Doric, Ionic, and Corinthian. Doric temples, such as those at Paestum, were characterized by sturdy plain columns. The more delicate Ionic order had columns with raised narrow bands, topped by a pair of scrolls. The most decorative order, the Corinthian, had columns topped with acanthus leaves.

◄ The temple of the goddess Hera, at Paestum in southern Italy, was built in about 550 B.C.E. It is one of the best preserved Greek temples anywhere.

Latins and Etruscans

The Romans were just one of the Latin-speaking peoples living in western Italy, in the area known as Latium. From 700 years B.C.E., the Etruscans, whose civilization dominated northern Italy, had the greatest influence on Latium. The Etruscans lived in wealthy cities, ruled by kings. They were experts at bronze **casting**, particularly figures of animals.

The Romans adopted many Etruscan customs, such as the wearing of a robe called a **toga**. In the 500s B.C.E., Rome was ruled by a series of kings of Etruscan descent, the last of whom was driven out in the year 510 or 509 B.C.E.

Better than the Greeks?

When it came to art, the Romans always felt inferior to the Greeks. At the same time, they were proud that they had been able to unite the previously disunited Greeks by bringing them into their **empire**. In his *Aeneid*, the Roman poet Vergil contrasted the "arts" of foreign peoples, such as Greeks, with those of Rome:

"There will be others to beat the breathing bronze with greater skill and grace. Others too will draw out living faces from the marble ... But you, Roman, must remember that you have to guide the nations by your authority. These are your arts: to bring the ways of peace, to show mercy to the conquered, and to crush the proud."

▼ This Etruscan sarcophagus (stone coffin) shows a ceremony called a *conclamatio* (shouting together), a custom used by Greeks, Etruscans, and Romans when mourning their dead.

The mourners cry out the name of the dead woman.

They hold flasks of perfumed oil, used to anoint the dead.

The body is laid out on a couch.

Even the dog is in mourning for its mistress.

The Republic

After the last Etruscan king was driven out, around 509 B.C.E., Rome's government became a **republic**. Instead of being ruled by a king, Rome was governed by annually elected officials called **magistrates**. The most important were the two chief magistrates, called **consuls**. They were Rome's heads of state and the commanders of the armies. The consuls ruled with the advice of an assembly of approximately 600 serving and former magistrates, called the **Senate**.

Magistrates were attended in public by officials called *lictors,* who carried a bundle of rods with an axe in the middle, called a *fasces.* Originally an Etruscan symbol, this showed the power of the magistrate to punish offenders with death or a beating.

Voting

Every adult male **citizen** had the right to vote for the magistrates. Yet the work of a magistrate was unpaid, so only the wealthiest could afford to run for election. Rich families were also able to use their influence to get their candidates elected. As a result, most of the magistrates came from only a small number of wealthy families. Women, slaves, and noncitizens did not have the right to vote or to hold public office.

▼ A carved **relief** from around 100 B.C.E. shows a census being carried out. This was the updating of the register of citizens, to determine who had the right to vote, and what taxes people should pay.

The censor, a senior magistrate, records the names of citizens.

This man, identified as a citizen by his toga, has to state his name, age, occupation, amount of property, and the name of his father.

He carries a document, perhaps a grant of citizenship.

Shirt of mail, or iron rings—the plate armor shown on Trajan's column had not yet been invented.

This Roman soldier provides good evidence for the armor worn in 100 B.C.E.

Toga

Only male citizens could wear a **toga**—a large semicircle of cloth, about 23 feet (7 meters) long and 10 feet (3 meters) wide. Sculptures of men in togas help us discover how these were worn, draped in complicated folds around the body, covering the left arm while leaving the right arm free.

The usual toga was made of undyed wool. A toga *praetexta*, with a purple border, was worn by certain magistrates and boys from noble families, while a black toga *pulla* was worn for funerals. Men running for election wore a toga *candida*, whitened with chalk (this is where we get our word "candidate"). Generals in triumphal processions wore a purple toga *picta*, embroidered with gold palm leaves. Beneath the toga a Roman wore a tunic—those worn by senators were decorated with a broad purple stripe.

Although it was heavy and awkward, wearing a toga was a sign of respectability, like a suit and tie today. When foreigners were granted Roman citizenship, one of the first things they had to do was to learn how to wear a toga.

▶ The custom of wearing a toga meant a great deal of work for ancient sculptors, forced to recreate every fold of the cloth. This bronze statue, dating from 90 B.C.E., shows a magistrate named Aulus Metellus making a speech.

The left arm is covered by the toga.

The right arm is left free to make gestures while giving the speech—even left-handed Romans were expected to use their right hands for writing and eating.

From the inscription on the base, we learn that this statue of an Etruscan citizen of Rome was set up by his sons to honor him after death.

A Roman career

In the 100 years B.C.E., the life of a Roman politician followed a set path, called the *cursus honorum* (path of honor). After spending his twenties in the army, a man could run for election as a *quaestor* when he reached the age of 30. There were 20 *quaestors*, responsible for collecting taxes and spending public money. The next stage, at the age of 39, was to be made a *praetor*, one of Rome's dozen or more judges. At the age of 42, a man could run for the consulship, the highest honor available to any Roman.

Conquering the Empire

The Roman **Empire** was conquered little by little. From 400 to 270 B.C.E., the Romans fought wars against other Italian peoples, eventually becoming the dominant power in the country. Rome was then drawn into three wars with the people of Carthage, in North Africa, whose own empire included Sicily and southern Spain. Carthage was finally defeated and destroyed in 146 B.C.E. In the same period, Roman armies were campaigning in the east, conquering Greece and Syria.

The conquests in the east led to vast amounts of treasure being brought back to Rome. This included many famous Greek paintings and statues, carried in triumphal processions and then used to decorate temples and other public buildings.

▼ This is just one small scene from Trajan's column, yet it is packed with information. It tells us about the Roman army, and also about the enemy Dacians, one of whom can be seen at the bottom left.

Roman armies

Success in warfare was due to the **discipline** and skill of the legionaries—**citizen** soldiers who wore heavy armor and fought on foot. Each legionary carried a large shield and a short stabbing sword called a *gladius*. The soldiers trained to march and fight in tight ranks, obeying signals from trumpeters. They followed **standard-**bearers who carried golden eagles and other religious symbols on long poles. These images were treated as sacred objects, and it was a disgrace to lose them in battle.

Like soldiers in modern armies, Roman soldiers dressed alike, wearing red tunics beneath their identical armor. The shields of each legion were decorated with the same images, such as thunderbolts and eagles. This helped the men think of themselves as a group, rather than individuals, and made them better fighters.

The figures march up the column, from left to right, as if the column is a mountain that the army is climbing.

This line where two of the column's drums joined together shows that the carving was done after the column was erected.

The helmets have small rings on top, so they could be hung from a cord over the shoulder when they were not worn.

A captured Dacian, with beard, cloak, and long trousers

The standards were decorated with various images, including wreaths (prizes for victory) and portraits of the emperor.

This standard with a square flag on top was called a vexillum; it carried the legion's number and name.

The shields are decorated with eagles' wings and lightning bolts, both emblems of Jupiter, the sky god and protector of Rome.

The men's big muscles show how fit they were, due to constant exercise such as long marches carrying heavy equipment.

Alongside the legionaries, there were lighter-armed noncitizen soldiers, called auxiliaries, including archers from Syria and slingers from Spain. After serving for 25 years as an auxiliary, a retiring soldier would be rewarded with Roman citizenship. Roman soldiers were kept constantly busy, going on long marches carrying heavy equipment. When they were not fighting or training for war, they often had to build roads. These helped the armies move quickly from one part of the empire to another.

Sharing citizenship

The great secret of Roman success was that, unlike other ancient peoples, they were willing to share their citizenship. The right to be a Roman citizen was given not just to retiring auxiliaries, but also to the ruling classes of conquered lands, or to individuals as a reward for loyal service. This gave the conquered peoples a stake in the Roman Empire.

▼ This map shows the growth of the Roman Empire from 14 C.E. until 117, when it reached its largest size. For the only time in history, all these different lands were united under the rule of one people.

▶ This carving, from a triumphal arch at Carpentras in Gaul (France), commemorates campaigns against the Germans and Dalmatians in 13–9 B.C.E. The fact that it was built in Gaul shows that the local people had come to see themselves as Romans.

Slavery

Carvings celebrating Roman victories often show defeated enemies in chains. Their fate would be slavery—being bought and sold as property and forced to work in quarries and mines and on farming estates. When we look at a Roman building, such as a temple, we should remember that the stones used to make it were often quarried by slaves captured in warfare, working long hours in terrible conditions.

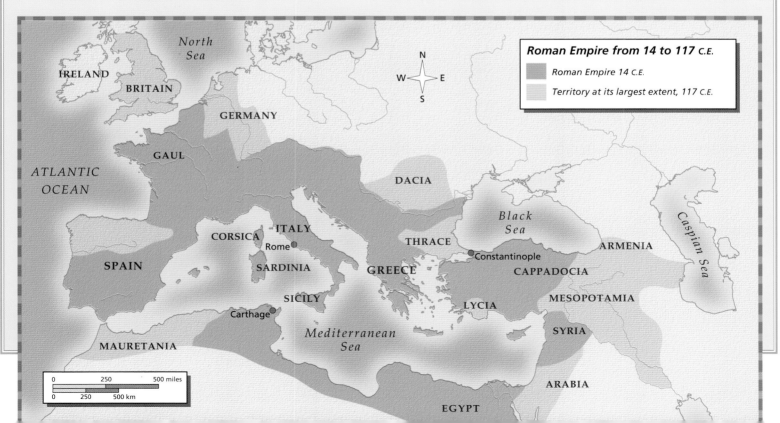

Roman Empire from 14 to 117 C.E.

Roman Empire 14 C.E.

Territory at its largest extent, 117 C.E.

North Sea

IRELAND

BRITAIN

GERMANY

GAUL

ATLANTIC OCEAN

DACIA

Black Sea

ITALY

CORSICA

Rome

THRACE

Constantinople

ARMENIA

Caspian Sea

SPAIN

SARDINIA

GREECE

CAPPADOCIA

SICILY

LYCIA

MESOPOTAMIA

Carthage

Mediterranean Sea

SYRIA

MAURETANIA

ARABIA

EGYPT

0   250   500 miles
0   250   500 km

Civil Wars

The republican system broke down in the 100 years B.C.E., when a series of **ambitious** generals used their armies to take control of the state. For men like Julius Caesar and his rival, Pompey, to be **consul** for a year was no longer enough. They wanted lasting power.

Caesar and Pompey

In 49 B.C.E., Julius Caesar, the conqueror of Gaul (France), quarreled with Pompey, who dominated the **Senate**. When Pompey ordered Caesar to disband his army and return to Rome, Caesar refused. **Civil war** erupted. Caesar led his army into Italy and seized power. Pompey fled east with the rest of the senators to gather his forces. Caesar pursued them and, in 48 B.C.E., defeated Pompey, who was later murdered. Caesar then began to behave like a king, issuing coins with his own portrait, an honor previously given only to dead Romans. In 44 B.C.E., he was murdered by a group of 60 senators, desperate to save the **republic**.

◄ Pompey was a plump man with a round face who looked nothing like Alexander the Great. This did not stop him imitating the famous king, as this bust shows.

This hairstyle, copied from Alexander the Great, was called anastole in Greek.

Pompey tilts his head to one side, a gesture often adopted by Alexander the Great in busts.

► Copies of busts of Alexander the Great could be seen all over the Roman Empire. Alexander's face would have been as familiar to people then as any film star is to us today. Note the brushed-up central forelocks, copied by Pompey.

Imitating Alexander

The great role model for Roman generals was King Alexander the Great of Macedonia, who had conquered a vast empire during the 300s B.C.E., before dying at the age of only 32. As a young man, Julius Caesar wept at the sight of a statue of Alexander—it reminded him of how little he had achieved in comparison with Alexander. Caesar's rival, Pompey, modeled himself on Alexander. Following his conquest of Syria, Pompey was given the right to call himself "the Great," like Alexander. Statues show that he even adopted Alexander's hairstyle, with locks brushed up high from the forehead, like a lion's mane.

Octavian and Antony

Caesar's great-nephew and adopted son, Octavian, and his friend Mark Antony then seized power in Rome. After defeating Caesar's killers in battle, they shared the Roman **Empire** between them, with Antony ruling the east and Octavian the west. It was not long before Antony and Octavian also fought. In 31 B.C.E., Octavian defeated Antony and his partner, Cleopatra, queen of Egypt, at the sea battle of Actium. Antony and Cleopatra both killed themselves, leaving Octavian the sole ruler of the Roman world.

The first emperor

In 27 B.C.E., Octavian announced that he was restoring power to the Senate. He claimed that from that time on, he would simply be Rome's *princeps* (first man). Although this gesture won him popularity, he did not give up any real power. He decided who could become a senator or consul, and he kept control of the armies. Renamed Augustus ("the honored one"), he had become Rome's first emperor. People were grateful to Augustus for bringing peace after years of civil war. During his reign, lasting for more than 40 years, the Romans got used to being ruled by only one man.

▼ This silver coin of Julius Caesar was issued in 44 B.C.E., the year of his murder.

Previously, only generals in triumphal processions wore laurel wreaths, but the Senate delighted Caesar by giving him the right to wear one at all times—allowing him to hide his baldness.

This type of silver coin is called a denarius.

No attempt is made to hide the lines on Caesar's scrawny neck—a typically unflattering Roman coin portrait.

The Image of Augustus

Augustus wanted people to think of him as the protector of the **empire**, who had brought peace after years of bitter **civil war**, and who was favored by the gods of Rome. He saw that the best way to get this message across was through art.

Although Augustus ruled the empire for 44 years, his statues and coin portraits always showed him as a handsome young man. In these statues, he appears in various roles. Sometimes he is a general giving commands, and at other times he is a priest, his head covered as a sign of respect for the gods. Sometimes he appears seminaked, following the Greek tradition of representing godlike heroes in this way.

The Prima Porta Augustus

The most famous statue of Augustus was found in 1963 at Prima Porta, to the north of Rome. Augustus is dressed as a general wearing a decorated breastplate. At its center, a man from Parthia, a powerful eastern kingdom, hands over a **standard** to a Roman soldier. The scene celebrates a treaty that Augustus made in 20 B.C.E. with the Parthians, in which they agreed to return standards they had captured following a victory over Rome in 53 B.C.E. Augustus claimed that he had forced the Parthians to return the standards and turned the earlier defeat into a great victory. Around this scene, the gods watch approvingly.

▼ The Prima Porta statue of Augustus, carved from marble, stands 6.7 ft. (2.03 m) high.

A Parthian returns one of the captured standards.

Shoulder clasps decorated with mythical creatures called sphinxes; Augustus used a sphinx on his seal.

The Earth goddess holds a cornucopia (horn of plenty) filled with fruit, showing that Augustus has provided peace and plenty to the empire.

Cupid (son of Venus, goddess of love) riding a dolphin.

In art, bare feet, like nakedness, were signs of a godlike hero.

The artist has done a wonderful job of carving the military commander's cloak, or paludamentum.

By Augustus' right foot, there is a figure of Cupid (the son of Venus, goddess of love). Cupid rides a dolphin, recalling Venus' birth from the sea. This is a reminder of Augustus' claim that his own family was descended from Venus.

Augustus

We can compare the statue of Augustus with a description of him by his biographer, Suetonius:

*"Augustus' eyes were clear and bright, and he liked to believe that they shone with a sort of **divine** radiance ... His teeth were small, few, and decayed; his hair yellowish and rather curly; his eyebrows met above the nose ... His body is said to have been marred by blemishes of various sorts ... and a number of hard dry patches suggesting ringworm."*

Coins

Augustus used his coins as miniature newspapers, to announce his achievements and to spread information. One side carried his portrait, together with his titles, such as "Pater Patriae" (father of the country). The reverse had a picture, possibly showing a newly completed temple, with a short slogan. Typical slogans are: "He restored the laws and rights of the Roman people," and "Roads have been built."

▲ This gold coin of Augustus shows his grandsons, Gaius and Lucius, whom he adopted as his sons and heirs. He intended that they rule after him, and used coins to get people used to the idea.

▼ The Ara Pacis is an altar to the goddess of peace, built in 13–9 B.C.E. by Augustus to show that he had brought peace after the long civil wars.

Aeneas, a legendary ancestor of Augustus, sacrifices a sow to the Penates, the gods who watched over Latium. Aeneas had just reached Latium after fleeing the city of Troy, sacked by the Greeks.

This badly damaged panel once showed Romulus and Remus with their father Mars and the shepherd who found them with the she-wolf.

The interior is decorated with garlands and ox skulls, representing sacrifice to the gods.

Mars, god of war

Faustulus, the shepherd

The lower level is richly decorated with intertwined acanthus plants in full flower, as well as birds, small animals, and insects—showing that even nature is flourishing thanks to Augustus' wise rule.

The City of Rome

B y the year 100 C.E., Rome was the world's largest city, with a population of more than a million people. Its center was filled with grand public buildings, including temples, theaters, amphitheaters, race tracks, and **basilicas** (halls used as law courts and for public meetings). There were also dozens of big public bathhouses. Romans saw their city as the center of the world.

▲ Here you can see what remains of the Emperor Caracalla's vast bathhouse in Rome. This is one of the baths' great halls that would once have been crowded with Romans relaxing and admiring art.

▼ In bathhouses all over the **empire**, a common subject for mosaics was the sea god Neptune. This mosaic comes from Besançon, France.

Neptune can be identified by his trident (three-pronged fishing spear).

Real horses pull his chariot—in many mosaics, it is pulled by hippocampi (fish-tailed horses).

In each corner, there is a hippocampus.

A dolphin, with its beaklike nose

Bathhouses

One of the largest of Rome's bathhouses was built by Caracalla, who was emperor from 211 to 217 C.E. It covered 27 acres (11 hectares) and could hold around 1,600 people at one time. This was much more than a place to wash. Caracalla's baths included gardens, restaurants, a gymnasium for exercise, a swimming pool, a running track, and libraries. The bathhouse was also an art gallery—its halls were lined with big marble statues, mostly copies of famous Greek works. The walls were lined with beautiful multicolored stone panels, such as purple porphyry from Egypt. **Mosaics**, showing gods and mythical sea creatures, covered the floors.

People went to the baths in the afternoons to relax, exercise, and meet friends. Caracalla built his bathhouse in order to make himself popular with the people of Rome. It cost very little to visit, so even the poorest **citizens** could afford to go. The emperor also wanted to leave the city a great monument that would outdo the bathhouses of earlier emperors.

Central heating

The baths used a central heating system, called a *hypocaust,* that passed hot air from a furnace through spaces behind walls and beneath floors. Different rooms were heated to different temperatures. There was one *sudatorium* (sweating room) that used dry heat, like a sauna, and another that used steam. In these warm rooms, people were massaged by slaves, who rubbed their bodies with scented oil, and scraped them clean with a metal tool called a *strigil.* The bathhouse also had cold rooms, with refreshing plunge baths.

▼ Every large city needed aqueducts to bring water for the baths. This wonderfully preserved example, 2,950 feet (900 meters) long, can be seen in Segovia, Spain.

Water supply

The city of Rome required a vast water supply, carried from the surrounding hills along eleven huge **aqueducts**. Water constantly flowed along the aqueducts into the bathhouses, holding tanks, street fountains, public toilets, and sewers, so that these were continually flushed. According to the Greek writer Strabo, so plentiful was Rome's water supply that "rivers flow through the city and the sewers."

Practical values

Frontinus (c. 35 C.E.–104) was the official responsible for maintaining Rome's water supply. He proudly contrasted the usefulness of his aqueducts with the famous tombs and temples of the Greeks and Egyptians: *"I ask you! Just compare with the vast monuments of this vital **aqueduct** network those useless pyramids, or the good-for-nothing tourist attractions of the Greeks."*

At this point, the aqueduct is 115 feet (35 meters) high.

The upper level has to be at exactly the right angle to ensure a constant flow of water from the hills to the city.

The use of arches allowed the Romans to build on a vast scale.

It was built using large granite blocks, the best local building material.

Roman Architecture

"In great buildings, as well as in other things, the rest of the world has been outdone by us Romans," boasted Pliny the Elder, a Roman writer. One reason for their ability to create great buildings was the Romans' invention of concrete, something easy to make and use. Roman concrete was made of rubble mixed with mortar made from lime (burnt chalk or limestone), volcanic ash, and water. The mortar hardened as it dried, holding the concrete together, and the rubble gave the concrete its strength. Lower parts of walls had to bear the most weight and were made with heavy stone rubble, while ceilings used light pumice rubble.

▼ The tallest building in ancient Rome was the Colosseum, a vast **amphitheater** built by the Emperor Vespasian and his son, Titus, in 72–80 C.E. Its ruined state helps us to see how it was constructed.

The other main Roman building material was brick, **mass-produced** in vast quantities. Unlike a Greek temple, built with carved stones, a typical Roman temple was made of concrete and brick. Stone was saved for the skin of the building.

Arches

Roman builders made great use of the arch, a curved structure spanning an open space. A wall using arches is as strong as a solid one, but much quicker to build. It is also lighter, so it does not require such deep foundations. Arches were used to build **aqueducts** and the outer walls of large theaters and amphitheaters. The Romans also invented triumphal arches, decorative gateways built as monuments and used for victory processions.

The walls' cores are made of brick and concrete.

The walls were covered with gray limestone, brought from a quarry 10.6 miles (17 kilometers) north of Rome.

These arches once held statues of gods and heroes.

The Colosseum had 76 different entrances, to allow an audience of up to 50,000 people to enter and leave quickly and safely.

Vaults and domes

An arch could be extended to make a barrel vault (a rounded ceiling shaped like half a cylinder). A number of arches, rotated in a circle, could also be used to make a dome, another wonderful Roman invention. For the first time, a large interior space could be created without needing dozens of columns to support the ceiling.

Slave labor

A tomb carving belonging to a family called the Haterii, who may have been building contractors, is useful evidence for construction methods. It shows the building of a large tomb resembling a temple. The scene includes a huge crane raised by men, possibly slaves, walking inside a wheel. Thanks to slavery, Roman builders had a ready supply of cheap labor, another reason for their ability to build such vast structures.

▼ This carving, from the tomb of the family of Quintus Haterius Tychicus, is one of the few Roman images of building work in progress.

These men on top of the crane show that Roman building work must have been very dangerous.

Crane used to lift heavy blocks of stone

Roof covered with terra-cotta tiles

A portrait of the dead woman, one of the family buried in the tomb, is in the pediment, the space on a temple usually kept for statues of gods.

Corinthian columns topped with Jupiter's sacred eagles

Portraits of dead members of the Haterii family

A wheel powered by men walking inside

A portrait of the dead woman shown in the temple pediment

Portraits of deceased family members

Pantheon

The most famous Roman dome is that of the Pantheon, a temple to all the gods built in Rome by the emperor Hadrian between 118 C.E. and 125. It is made of concrete, with 140 square coffers (recesses). These are decorative, but also help to reduce the ceiling's weight. An opening at the top, called an *oculus* (eye), lets a beam of light stream in. Throughout the day, this beam moves around the walls, illuminating the spaces where statues of the gods once stood. Most ancient temples were designed to be seen from the outside. The Pantheon is one of the earliest buildings whose interior is even more impressive than its exterior. It has been continuously used as a place of worship ever since it was built.

Sculpture

Ancient books provide the names of dozens of sculptors who worked for the Romans. Almost all of them were Greeks, who had a long tradition of carving marble into statues and **reliefs**.

Carving

A sculptor used different tools at different stages of his work. The rough work at the beginning was done with a big hammer and heavy chisel, as well as a bow drill—a metal drill that got started spinning by using a bow. Finer chisels with flat, curved, and toothed blades were better suited for the delicate work.

Although Roman statues seem plain today, surviving traces of paint show that they looked very different when they were made. Details such as the eyes and hair were brightly painted to give them a lifelike appearance. They were also polished with wax, to preserve and heighten their colors.

Marble

The most prized stone used in Roman sculpture was white marble, with its sparkling surface and fine grain. It could be cut into sharp details and polished to give it a smooth surface. Until the year 100 C.E., marble had to be imported from Greece and Asia Minor (modern-day Turkey). Then the Romans discovered a new source, in the Carrara mountains of northern Italy.

Colored marble was also used, such as porphyry, a purple stone from the Egyptian desert. In statues of emperors, sculptors might combine different marbles, using porphyry for the body, draped in a **toga** or wearing armor, and white marble for the head.

The head is made of white Carrara marble.

The lines show Caracalla as a troubled, serious man.

These eyes would once have been painted.

The marble has been finely polished.

The emperor wears armor made from porphyry, from Egypt.

▶ This marble bust is Emperor Caracalla (ruled 211–217 C.E.) who built the baths shown on page 18. A ruthless man, Caracalla murdered his own brother and coruler. He was eventually assassinated.

Bronze making

Bronze statues, such as those of emperors on horseback, were made by a complicated method called the "lost wax" process. First, a sculptor made a rough clay model of the work. This was used to make a clay "master mold." Melted wax was then poured into the mold. After carefully removing the mold to be used again, the wax model was given fine details. This was then encased in clay, making a second mold that was then baked, so that the wax melted and poured out through vents (holes). A pair of men used tongs to lift a **crucible** (melting pot) filled with **molten** bronze, and poured it into the mold. The bronze that filled the space left by the "lost wax" was then allowed to cool and harden. Finally, the mold was smashed open.

Since two men could lift only a small amount of molten bronze, statues had to be made in small pieces that were later fitted together. Despite this, artists were able to make enormous bronze statues, called colossi. The most famous was a statue of Emperor Nero that stood at the entrance to the emperor's palace. It was over 100 feet (30 meters) high, and was so heavy that it required the strength of 24 elephants when it was later moved to make way for a new temple.

▼ This larger than life-size bronze head of the emperor Augustus was found buried beneath the steps of a temple at Meroe, Sudan. It was probably taken there by raiders who attacked Roman Egypt in 25–21 B.C.E.

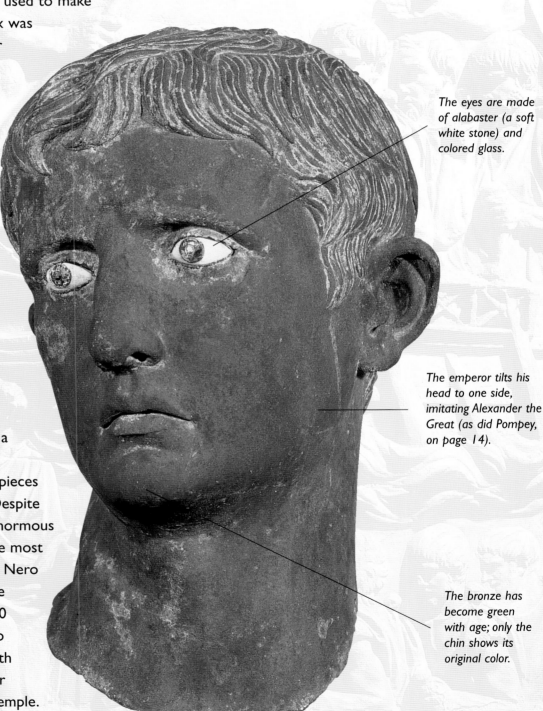

The eyes are made of alabaster (a soft white stone) and colored glass.

The emperor tilts his head to one side, imitating Alexander the Great (as did Pompey, on page 14).

The bronze has become green with age; only the chin shows its original color.

23

Public Shows

The biggest Roman buildings were those designed for public shows—"circuses," or tracks for chariot racing, and amphitheaters. An **amphitheater** was a circular or oval open-air building, where men called gladiators fought to the death to entertain vast cheering crowds. These shows were staged, at great expense, by Rome's ruling classes, as a way of winning popularity.

Pictures of the shows

Art helps us to understand what went on in these buildings, and also demonstrates just how popular the shows were. All over the **empire**, people decorated their homes with **mosaics** and wall paintings showing gladiator fights and chariot races. The same scenes also appear on everyday items, such as vases, oil lamps, and cutlery. Even babies' bottles had gladiators pictured on them. It was thought that the baby would drink in the gladiator's strength with the milk.

A favorite scene in art is the moment of victory, when one gladiator has wounded his opponent, who is no longer able to defend himself. The defeated gladiator is shown raising a finger, meaning that he was asking for mercy. The crowd would then shout, "Let him live!" or "Finish him off!" depending on how bravely he had fought.

Although gladiators were usually slaves or criminals, they were treated like athletes or pop stars today. They had many adoring fans, who wrote **graffiti** praising their heroes, such as this line found on a wall in Pompeii: Celadus the Thracian makes the girls sigh."

The mosaic may show two separate fights, or two stages of the same fight.

The Latin text says, "Astyanax conquers."

The wounded Kalendio appeals to the crowd for mercy.

This symbol represents death and defeat.

Kalendio has thrown his net over Astyanax.

Kalendio thrusts at Astyanax's legs with his trident.

The men in white are referees.

◀ This Spanish mosaic records a contest between two real gladiators, named Astyanax and Kalendio. Kalendio was a *retiarus*, a fighter armed with a net and trident. Astyanax was a *secutor*, or pursuer, armed with shield and sword.

Scorpus

The poet Martial wrote a poem commemorating the death of Scorpus, the charioteer:

"I am Scorpus, the glory of the noisy Circus,
The much-applauded and short-lived
darling of Rome.
Envious Fate, counting my victories
instead of my years,
And so believing me old,
Carried me off in my twenty-sixth year."

◄ This bronze household ornament shows a chariot pulled by a team of two galloping horses. The most popular chariot races had four-horse chariots.

Executions

Mosaics show another entertainment staged in amphitheaters—public executions. Criminals were tied to stakes to be torn apart by wild beasts, such as lions and tigers. The fact that it was acceptable to decorate homes with such scenes shows how bloodthirsty Roman tastes were. People believed that it was a good thing to kill criminals, and they enjoyed watching it done.

▼ Wild beast fights were sometimes held in the circus (racetrack), as in this terra-cotta (pottery) plaque. We know that this is a racetrack because of the seven egg-shaped objects in the middle, used to record laps of a race.

Chariot racing

Chariot racing was almost as dangerous as fighting in the amphitheater. Tomb inscriptions show that many charioteers died in their 20s, killed when their chariots overturned or crashed. A charioteer tied his horses' reins around his waist, so if he was thrown out of his chariot he was liable to be dragged to his death.

In the 100s C.E., the most famous charioteer in Rome was Scorpus, whose face was said to be painted on walls all over the city. Scorpus won 2,048 races before he was killed, at the age of just 26.

These were lowered as each lap of a chariot race was completed.

An excited spectator looks down from the safety of the front row.

This man is a bestiarius, a fighter who specialized in combat with wild animals.

Wild animals were often terrified by the shows, and had to be forced to fight, such as this lion being driven toward the bestiarius.

The fact that this dying man is naked suggests that he is not a gladiator but a condemned criminal, thrown to the beasts to be executed.

Trade and Crafts

Roman rule brought peace to all the lands around the Mediterranean Sea. The area was also cleared of pirates, making it safer for merchant ships to cross the seas carrying goods, such as grain from Africa, olive oil from Spain, and tin from Britain. Goods were also transported along rivers of the **empire** by barge.

Ships

Roman merchant ships were big-bellied vessels with large holds, making them stable but slow. Paintings, **mosaics**, coin images, and carved **reliefs** help us to understand how they were sailed. There were two square sails that could be used only with a following wind. Images in art also show us how merchant ships were decorated, with a lucky carved figure of a goose or swan's neck and head at the stern.

A Titanic of its time

The biggest ships were those of the grain fleet. One was described by the Greek writer, Lucian:
"What a tremendous vessel it was! 180 feet [55 meters] long, as the ship's carpenter told me, and more than a quarter of this across … And how the stern rose in a graceful curve ending in a gilt goose head, in harmony with the equal curve of the bow and the forepost with its picture of Isis, the goddess who had given the ship her name. All was unbelievable: the decoration, paintings, red topsail … And the whole fortune of the ship is in the hands of a little old man who moves the great rudders with a tiller no thicker than a stick."

▼ This crudely made black and white mosaic shows a typical merchant ship, with its two sails and steering oars.

This is the base of a Roman lighthouse.

Small foresail at the prow (front)

There was one large, square mainsail.

A very simple representation of a ship's figurehead, perhaps a winged goddess

The ship is steered with a pair of oars at the stern (rear); the stern rudder had not been invented.

Roman glass

In the 100 years B.C.E., glassmakers in Syria invented a new technique—glassblowing. A glassmaker blew through an iron pipe to inflate a lump of **molten** glass, then shaped it by spinning and rolling. Using this technique, they could make vases with layers of glass in different colors, such as a white layer on top of a dark blue layer. The outer layer was then cut away to make a relief picture called a cameo. Only thirteen complete glass cameo vases survive today. The best known is the Portland Vase, dating from the time of Augustus (27 B.C.E.–14 C.E.).

Samian ware

One trade item found on archaeological sites all over the Roman Empire, is Samian ware, a beautiful type of bright red pottery decorated with reliefs. It was mostly made in Gaul (France), where it was **mass-produced** in large workshops. It was manufactured by pushing clay into a stone mold that had been carved with patterns and pictures. We know the names of many potters, because they stamped them on their bowls.

◀ The Portland Vase is one of the most famous Roman works of art. The vase was intact until 1845, when it was smashed into 200 pieces. It has been repaired three times since then. Its subject is still disputed, but it is likely that it shows the courtship of the Greek sea nymph Thetis by the legendary king Peleus. Their child would be the famous hero, Achilles.

It is almost 10 in. (25 cm) high.

The white outer layer was carefully cut away to reveal the dark blue background.

The winged figure of Cupid, whose arrows cause people to fall in love

Peleus, king of Phthia in Thessaly, lays hold of Thetis.

The sea nymph Thetis

This may be the Greek sea god, Poseidon (Neptune), or his brother Zeus (Jupiter).

Family Life

In the 100s C.E., a Roman lawyer named Gaius wrote, "No other peoples have such power over their children as we have." He was talking about the power of the "paterfamilias" (father of the family), who headed every Roman family. The paterfamilias had complete power over his children, daughters-in-law, and grandchildren. Even when his sons were grown up, they had to wait until he died to become heads of families in their own right.

We still have many sculptures of elderly Roman men who must have been the heads of families. These are often unflattering, with wrinkles, double chins, and even warts. Even after death, a paterfamilias remained an important family member, remembered through his portrait or through a mask of him, displayed in the home and worn at funerals.

Family masks

The Greek writer Polybius described the Roman custom of wearing masks of dead family members at funerals:

"When any distinguished member of the family dies, the masks are taken to the funeral, and are there worn by men who are considered to bear the closest resemblance to the original … It would be hard to imagine a more impressive scene for a young man who aspires to win fame and to practice virtue. For who could remain unmoved at the sight of the images of all these men, who have won renown in their time, now gathered together as if alive and breathing?"

▼ A Roman paterfamilias, dressed in his best **toga**, proudly holds two portrait busts of his ancestors, perhaps his father and grandfather.

Although the statue dates from the first 100 years C.E., he has the closely cropped hair of the republican period, indicating that he is an old-fashioned believer in traditional values.

The toga is beautifully carved.

The figure is life-size, standing 5.4 feet (1.65 meters).

Trunk of a palm tree helps to support the sculpture.

◀ This richly carved **relief** shows a Roman marriage scene with a religious procession, on the left, and a **sacrifice**. The ceremony was overseen by a respectable older married woman, known as the *pronuba* (matron of honor).

The bride's head is covered with a flame-colored headscarf called a flammeum.

A sheep is brought to be sacrificed to the gods, to bring good luck.

The man whose head is covered with his toga is the priest in charge of the sacrifice.

The bride and groom join hands, watched over by the matron of honor.

To be chosen to be a pronuba, a woman had to be married and still living with her first husband.

Her dress was white, like those worn today by many Western brides.

Marriage

Marriages were arranged by the paterfamilias of the groom's and bride's families. In early times, a bride passed from her father's control to that of her husband or his father. By 100 years B.C.E., it was more usual for a wife to remain under the authority of her father or some other guardian. In practice, this meant that she could keep her money and property separate from her husband's.

Women

Men expected their wives to raise children, to give orders to household slaves, and to spend their spare time spinning and weaving. Even the richest women, such as Agrippina and Antonia, granddaughters of Augustus, were taught to spin and weave.

Daughters were valued less than sons and did not even have their own names. Agrippina and Antonia were given female versions of their fathers' names, Agrippa and Mark Antony.

Despite these limitations, women could play a major role in public life. Rich women often ran their own businesses and served in temples as priestesses. The women of the imperial family exercised great power, through their influence over their husbands and sons. One of the most powerful people in Rome was Livia, wife of Augustus and mother of Tiberius, his successor. Tiberius often complained that his mother wanted to be coruler of the **empire**. He could not afford to ignore her advice. She had a forceful personality and, after 52 years married to Augustus, knew everything there was to know about being an emperor.

House and Garden

On August 24 in the year 79, Mount Vesuvius, a volcano in southern Italy, erupted. Two nearby Roman towns, Herculaneum and Pompeii, were buried under a deep layer of ash, boiling mud, and volcanic rocks. This terrible disaster led to the almost complete **preservation** of the two towns, now uncovered by archaeologists.

Today you can visit Pompeii and Herculaneum, and walk from room to room in a Roman house. While the outside walls are plain, those inside are richly decorated with **mosaics**, wall paintings, **reliefs** made of stucco (plaster), statues, and statuettes.

Atrium and triclinium

The greatest expense for a household was decorating the two most public rooms of the house, the *atrium* and the *triclinium*. The *atrium* was the entrance hall, where the family received visitors every morning. The *triclinium* was the dining room, used for dinner parties. The word *triclinium* ("three couches") comes from the Roman habit of eating while reclining on couches. Here there was often an elaborate floor mosaic that could be admired by the diners as they ate.

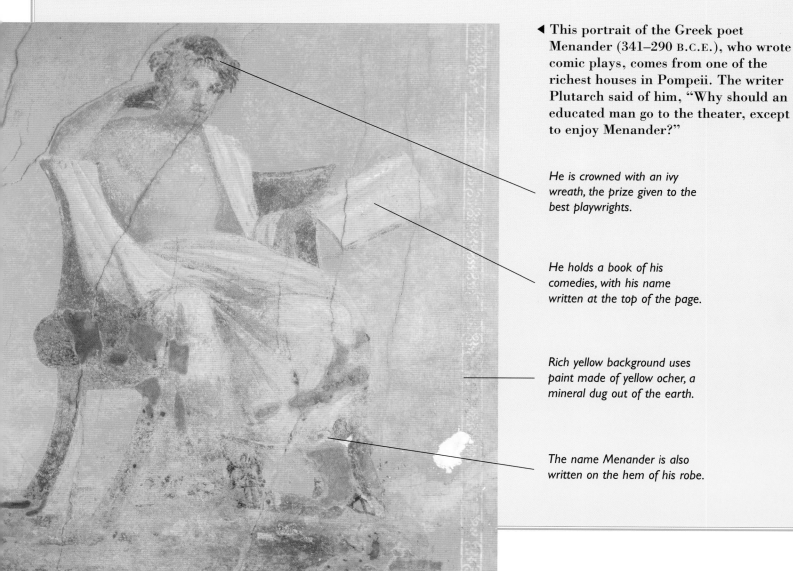

◄ This portrait of the Greek poet Menander (341–290 B.C.E.), who wrote comic plays, comes from one of the richest houses in Pompeii. The writer Plutarch said of him, "Why should an educated man go to the theater, except to enjoy Menander?"

He is crowned with an ivy wreath, the prize given to the best playwrights.

He holds a book of his comedies, with his name written at the top of the page.

Rich yellow background uses paint made of yellow ocher, a mineral dug out of the earth.

The name Menander is also written on the hem of his robe.

▶ This beautiful wall painting comes from a room in a house in Pompeii. It shows a nightingale singing in a garden full of flowers.

A tiny dot of white makes the nightingale's eye shine.

A laurel (bay) tree, sacred to Apollo

Red roses

Daisies

Wall paintings

Experts have identified different styles of wall painting, showing how fashions changed between 80 B.C.E. and 79 C.E. The earliest paintings imitate slabs of colored marble and other types of stone. Architectural features were added next, such as columns with painted shadows, creating an illusion of depth. The next stage was to add realistic paintings of landscapes between and behind the columns. In the last style, the architectural features became purely decorative. No attempt was now made to make columns which looked like real columns.

Fashion was continually changing, showing the importance of the home as a place to display wealth and good taste. Subjects of wall paintings were chosen for the same reasons. Paintings and mosaics of famous writers, such as the Greek playwright Menander and the Roman poet Vergil, showed a visitor how well educated the family was.

Gardens

The Romans loved gardens, and had garden scenes with spring flowers and birds painted on the inside walls of their homes. In the depths of winter, this was a reminder of the spring. Garden walls were also painted with outdoor scenes to make the gardens look bigger.

Gardener's world

The writer Pliny the Younger wrote a letter to a friend in which he lovingly described the garden of his country house: *"In front of the **colonnade** is a terrace laid out with box hedges clipped into different shapes ... with figures of animals cut out of the box ... In front is an ornamental pool, a pleasure both to see and hear, with its water falling from a height and foaming white when it strikes the marble ... Everywhere there is peace and quiet, which adds as much to the healthiness of the place as the clear sky and pure air."*

Mosaics

The best-known Roman art form is the **mosaic**—a picture made from tesserae (tiny pieces of pottery, stone, shell, or glass) set into mortar. While few Roman paintings outside Pompeii and Herculaneum have survived, we can still see thousands of mosaics from all over the Roman **Empire**. The reason is that mosaics were used on floors, often the only part of a Roman building to survive. Mosaics were also made to last. Before laying their tesserae, the craftsmen made sure that the floor had a firm foundation, using layers of rubble, crushed tile, and mortar, and pounding until the floor was level.

How were they made?

Simple patterns were made by placing tesserae directly into wet mortar. Complicated pictures were usually made in advance, either in a mosaic workshop or on the site. The tesserae might be laid in a tray of sand before a piece of glued cloth was placed on top. The whole picture was then lifted and placed onto the mortar. Once this had set, the cloth was soaked and peeled away. Gaps between the tesserae were filled, and the mosaic was cleaned and polished. In another method, the tesserae were glued directly onto the cloth, where the picture had first been drawn, in reverse.

The mosaic includes more than 1,500,000 tiny tesserae.

Alexander's horse was called Bucephalus ("ox head"), from its large head.

A forest of tall Macedonian pikes surrounds the king, who is being attacked from all sides.

Darius appears frozen in horror, his arm outstretched toward the Persian whom Alexander has just killed.

Darius's charioteer frantically whips the horses to escape from the battlefield.

The whole picture is 9 ft. by 17 ft. (2.7 m by 5.2 m).

Alexander is spearing a Persian nobleman, but his eyes are fixed on Darius, his true enemy.

The picture wonderfully captures the confusion and terror of a battlefield.

As his horse tumbles beneath him, the Persian is stabbed with Alexander's spear.

◄ The "Alexander mosaic" from Pompeii shows the turning point of the Battle of Issus in 333 B.C.E. Alexander the Great charged straight for the Persian king, who fled from the battlefield.

Patterns and pictures

Similar pictures and patterns appear in mosaics from different countries. This suggests that the craftsmen may have had catalogs with pictures of mosaics, to show to their clients for them to choose from. People could also select a mosaic reproduction of a famous painting. A mosaic from Pompeii in the first 100 years C.E. shows a battle between Alexander the Great of Macedonia and King Darius of Persia. This is a copy of a lost wall painting, made around 300 B.C.E. by a Greek artist called Philoxenos.

A famous mosaic

Pliny the Elder described an unusual mosaic that became a tourist attraction:

"The most celebrated worker in mosaic was Sosus, who at Pergamum laid the floor of what is known in Greek as the Asaraton Oecon ("Unswept Room") because, by means of small cubes tinted in various shades, he represented on the floor refuse from the dinner table and other sweepings, making them appear as if they had been left there."

▼This mosaic shows three birds drinking from a bowl of water, eyed from below by a hungry cat.

A pheasant

A dove, in reality much smaller than the other two birds

A ring-necked parakeet, with lovely green and red feathers

Birds and water

A popular subject for mosaics was birds, often shown drinking from a bowl of water. The writer Pliny the Elder described a mosaic by an artist called Sosus of Pergamum, depicting "a dove, which is drinking and casts the shadow of its head on the water, while others are sunning and preening themselves on the brim of a large drinking vessel."

The challenge for the artist was to make water look like water.

This cat may be a young leopard.

33

Burying the Dead

Some Romans believed in an afterlife, though there were different ideas about exactly where it was located. Some thought that the spirits of the dead remained near their graves, while others believed that they traveled to an underworld, deep in the Earth.

Tomb carvings

Every Roman hoped to be remembered after death. Members of the ruling classes would be remembered thanks to the statues of them, set up in public places. However, ordinary people had only one place where they could display their portrait in public—on their tombs. Some tombs have carved portraits of the dead, while others have **reliefs** showing scenes from their lives. Such reliefs include bakers making bread, a midwife helping at a birth, and mothers with their children. Like photographs today, these carvings helped surviving relatives remember their loved ones. They also give us some of our best evidence for daily life in ancient Rome.

▼ This carving comes from the tomb of a midwife, and shows her helping a rich woman give birth. This is a work in which birth and death are linked together.

The carving shows us that Roman women gave birth in a seated position.

The new mother gazes at her baby.

Household slaves with towels stand by.

The midwife is identifiable as the subject of the scene because she is the only figure looking out of the picture at the viewer, as if she is saying to a passerby, "This was my life."

The large baby looks back up at its mother.

Visiting the dead

The dead were buried in tombs outside the walls of towns, usually placed alongside the main roads where they could be easily seen by passersby and visited by relatives. Family members visited the grave on the dead person's birthday and during an annual festival of the dead, called Feralia, held in late February. They brought flowers, food, and wine, offering these as gifts to the spirits of the dead. The poorest Romans, who could not afford a tomb carving, often marked a grave with the neck of a pottery jar, placed in the earth. Wine was poured into the jar for the spirit, down in the underworld, to drink.

In Egypt, there was an ancient belief that a dead person's body had to be preserved—as a mummy wrapped in bandages—for the spirit to survive. Roman mummies from Egypt were given beautiful portraits of the dead person, painted on boards that were tied in place with linen cloth. These pictures have survived thanks to the dry desert air, and are the finest ancient portrait paintings still in existence.

▶ This is one of the mummy portraits from Roman Egypt. What we do not know is whether it was painted while its subject was still alive or after her death. What do you think?

Epitaphs

Tombs were often carved with an epitaph, which is writing addressed to a passerby that describes the dead person. Women's epitaphs show us the qualities that Roman men prized in their wives. The following epitaph is from a Roman tomb of the 100s B.C.E.:

"Visitor, what I have to say is not much, stand a moment and read. This tomb is not beautiful, but it is for a beautiful woman. Her parents gave her the name Claudia. She loved her husband with her whole heart. She bore two children, of whom she left one above ground, and buried the other beneath the earth. Her conversation was agreeable, her bearing pleasing. She stayed at home, she worked at her wool. I have finished speaking. You may go."

Large expressive eyes are typical of these mummy portraits.

She is probably wearing makeup—Roman women whitened their skin with cosmetics made from lead, not realizing that it was poisonous.

The artist painted on wood with encaustic paint (pigments mixed with beeswax).

Mummy portraits are good evidence for Roman jewelry, such as this woman's earrings and necklace.

Roman Religion

The Romans believed in hundreds of different gods, each responsible for different areas of life. The most important was Jupiter ("Best and Greatest"), the sky god. He was the special protector of the Roman **Empire**, and the emperor was his chief priest. It was the emperor's responsibility to offer prayers and gifts to Jupiter, to ensure his continued goodwill.

Sacrifice

Carved **reliefs** give us our best evidence for religious ceremonies. Here you can see Emperor Marcus Aurelius, whose statue on horseback we saw on page 6. The building in the background is the temple of Jupiter on Rome's Capitoline Hill. Behind its closed doors there was a huge seated statue of the god, made of terra cotta. Its great size conveyed the god's superhuman nature.

Marcus Aurelius is shown scattering incense onto a brazier, while saying a prayer that included the words, "Keep safe the state of the **citizens**, the people of Rome." The boy in the middle plays a pipe, in order to prevent Jupiter from hearing any words except the emperor's prayer. The bull standing behind will shortly be sacrificed, or killed as an offering to Jupiter. The killing will be done by the man who is stripped to the waist and carries an axe. Some of the bull's meat will then be burned on an altar, the rising smoke thought to carry the gift to the god.

▼ Rome's temple of Jupiter has not survived, so this carved relief of a sacrificial scene is useful evidence for what it looked like. You can see from the column tops that it was a Corinthian temple.

Bull to be sacrificed

Marcus Aurelius, head covered, acting as a priest

Brazier for burning sweet-smelling incense, another gift for the god

Boy piper

The sacrificer, holding his axe ready

The last stage of the ceremony was to examine the bull's liver. A healthy-looking liver was believed to be a sign that Jupiter was pleased with the **sacrifice**, and would answer the emperor's prayers. An emperor was expected to perform this ceremony before beginning any major undertaking, such as starting a war or building a new temple. The Romans firmly believed that nothing could be achieved without the help of their gods.

Vesta's priestesses

While male gods were served by male priests, female gods had priestesses. It was the special duty of the priestesses of Vesta, goddess of the hearth, to keep a sacred fire burning day and night. Priestesses of Vesta were forbidden to marry, yet they had many privileges, such as the best seats at public shows.

Household gods

Just as there were gods who protected the Roman Empire, every house and family had its own protective household gods. These included the Lares, who watched over the dividing lines between one household and another, and the Penates, who guarded the storerooms. Entrances to homes were the responsibility of three separate gods: Forculus, who protected the doors; Limentinus, who guarded the threshold; and Cardea, goddess of door hinges. The family made daily offerings of food and wine to small statues of their household gods.

▶ This is a household shrine, like a miniature temple, where the family kept the small statues of the gods who protected their home.

▼ This relief shows the goddess Vesta with four of her priestesses and an unidentified male figure.

Priestesses

*The **toga** tells us that this is a man, perhaps an emperor or important priest.*

Vesta

Emperor Worship

One strange aspect of Roman religion was that emperors were given **divine** honors, with their own temples, priests, and **sacrifices**. People made offerings to the genius (life force) of the living emperor, while some emperors, such as Augustus, were declared to have become gods after death. Few people believed that an emperor was a god in the same way that Jupiter was. They did not expect him to answer their prayers. Rather, emperor worship was a way of showing loyalty to the Roman state.

Attitudes toward being worshiped

Different emperors had different attitudes toward emperor worship. Caligula (ruled 37–41 C.E.), who was mentally ill, seems to have thought that he really was a god. According to his biographer, Suetonius, he liked to dress as Jupiter, with a golden beard and a thunderbolt, and stand in a temple, like a statue, to be worshiped. In contrast, a later emperor, Vespasian (ruled 79–81 C.E.), made a famous joke on his deathbed: "Dear me! I seem to be turning into a god!"

Becoming a god

The beautifully carved ivory panel on the left, dating from around 400 C.E., shows a funeral ceremony called a *consecratio* ("making sacred"), in which an emperor was thought to become a god. In the background you can see the emperor's funeral pyre, a tall wooden structure covered with purple cloth. On top there is a statue of a four-horse chariot, the type driven by generals in triumphal processions. This represented the emperor's victory over death.

◄ This little ivory, just 12 in. by 4⅓ in. (30 cm by 11 cm), is one of the last images made showing the old Roman religion. When it was carved, most Romans had become Christian.

A big statue of the emperor, now a god, sits in his temple on top of the carriage.

The two images of the eagle suggest its flight up from the pyre.

Elephants pull a great carriage in the funeral procession.

In early times, the body of the emperor was placed in the pyre, though later a wax image was used instead, so that people did not have to hunt though the ashes for the emperor's bones to place in his tomb. The pyre was set on fire, and an eagle was released from the topmost level. Its soaring flight represented the emperor's spirit flying up to join the other gods.

▼ This stone relief, showing Antonius Pius and his wife, Faustina, decorates one side of the base of a column, now lost. It shows us how the Romans imagined their emperors turning into gods.

Scepter topped with Jupiter's eagle

Eagles, representing the souls of the dead couple

Antonius Pius and Faustina

Roma, goddess of the city

This figure holding an Egyptian obelisk represents the area called the Campus Martius (Field of Mars).

Romulus and Remus are carved on the shield.

A winged god carries the couple up to heaven.

Up to heaven

Empresses as well as emperors were sometimes deified (made into gods). On the death of his wife Faustina, in 141 C.E., Emperor Antonius Pius (ruled 138–161) declared that she was a goddess and built a temple in her honor. When he died twenty years later, the temple was rededicated to both Antonius Pius and Faustina.

The emperor's successor, Marcus Aurelius, set up a **relief** carving (seen above) of the married couple, now

gods, flying up to heaven. They are carried by a winged figure and accompanied by two eagles, while two figures on the ground watch approvingly. The seated woman on the right has a shield decorated with a carving of Romulus and Remus, with their she-wolf. This tells us that she is Roma, goddess of the city of Rome. The man on the left holding an obelisk (an Egyptian column) represents an area called the Campus Martius, where an obelisk like this stood. It was in the Campus Martius that imperial funerals took place.

New Gods

As their **empire** grew, the Romans came across many foreign gods, most of whom were welcomed into the Roman religion. A number of Eastern gods, including Isis, from Egypt, and Mithras, from Persia (Iran), were worshiped in secret ceremonies. In order to take part, people underwent rites in which they were "initiated" (brought into the religion). Initiates had to make solemn promises never to reveal their ceremonies to outsiders.

Mystery religions, as they are called, offered people a more emotional religious experience than that provided by traditional Roman religion. Many used music and dance or a shared sacred meal to bring the worshipers closer to their god.

The Golden Ass

In a comic novel *The Golden Ass,* the writer Apuleius mockingly described a procession by Isis worshipers:

"The horn player struck up and they started brandishing enormous swords and maces and leaping about like maniacs ... Every now and then they would bite themselves savagely and ... cut their arms with the sharp knives that they carried. One of them let himself go more ecstatically than the rest. Heaving deep sighs from the very bottom of his lungs, as if filled with the spirit of the goddess, he pretended to go stark-mad."

▼ This wall painting from Pompeii shows Isis worshipers holding a ceremony in a garden in front of a temple.

The chief priest carries a golden vessel.

A priest and priestess shake sacred rattles, called sistra.

Egyptian sphinxes, lion figures with human heads

Several worshipers are black Africans.

The worshipers, wearing white linen robes, sing hymns praising their goddess.

A priest with a long baton conducts the singing.

Priests of Isis shaved their heads, following the ancient Egyptian custom.

A priest fans the flames on the altar.

Ibises, birds sacred to Isis

Mithras

Since the ceremonies of mystery religions took place in secret, art often provides our only source of evidence for them. Much of what we know of Mithras worship comes from more than a thousand pieces of sculpture, found across the empire. The commonest are carvings of the god in the act of killing a bull with a dagger. According to one view, by killing this bull, Mithras gave life to the Earth. Another idea is that the figures represent constellations in the night sky. Whatever this sculpture means, it occupied the most important place in every "Mithraeum," the dark hall where the god's initiates met to perform their mysterious ceremonies.

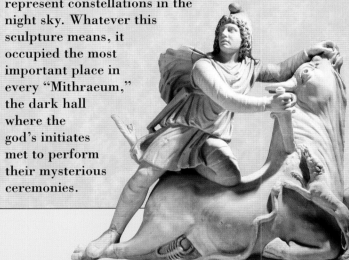

Christ

Christianity was another Eastern religion that spread across the empire in the first 200 years C.E. Christians worshiped Jesus Christ, a Jewish religious teacher executed by crucifixion (being nailed to a cross) in about 30 C.E. They believed that Jesus was the Son of God, who had risen from the dead and who promised eternal life to his followers.

Crucifixion was a painful and humiliating death reserved for slaves and rebels. The idea of worshiping someone who had been crucified baffled most Romans. From the emperor's point of view, the problem with Christians was their refusal to worship any Roman gods. Their failure to pay **divine** honors to the emperor was seen as treason. So Christians were often harshly persecuted, and were thrown to wild beasts in amphitheaters around the empire.

▼ This dark underground room is one of a dozen Mithraea found in Rome. It is thought to represent a sacred cave, where Mithras killed the bull.

Mithras worshipers sat on these long benches at the sides, eating a sacred meal.

The carving of the bull slaying is in the center.

Mithraea are always small, suggesting a limited number of worshipers.

Christianity

In the early 300s C.E., there was another series of **civil wars**, eventually won by Constantine, who was the sole emperor from 324 until 337. Constantine was a Christian, a follower of the religion forbidden by earlier emperors. He used his power to spread his religion, appointing Christians to important government posts, and building grand churches. He also created a new Christian capital for the **empire**, Constantinople.

Most of the emperors who followed Constantine were also Christians, and they made it more and more difficult to worship the old Roman gods. Under Theodosius (ruled 379–395), Christianity became the only permitted religion. Across the empire, Christians destroyed the old statues of the gods, believing them to be devils, and carved crosses on temple walls. Many temples were torn down, while others were converted into churches.

▶ This is the church of Hagia Sophia, now a museum in Istanbul.

Hagia Sophia

Unlike a temple, designed as a backdrop for open-air ceremonies, a church was a building for group worship. Therefore, the interior of a church was more important, and more richly decorated, than its exterior.

The greatest late Roman church is Hagia Sophia (Holy Wisdom) in Constantinople, built by Emperor Justinian in 532–537 C.E. It was described by the writer Procopius as a sight of "indescribable beauty ... full of light and sunshine."

Light streams through 40 arched windows that form a corona (crown).

Arabic text with the names of Allah and Muhammad, added when Constantinople was conquered by the Muslim Turks

The central dome is 102 ft. (31 m) across and 184 ft. (56 m) high.

The dome is supported by arches.

A Roman Christ

Although the old Roman religion was destroyed, Christianity took on many of its features. The roles of different gods were now played by saints. Instead of asking help from a goddess, such as Diana or Minerva, worshipers turned to Mary, the mother of Christ.

This **mosaic** from Ravenna, Italy in the 500s C.E., shows Christ wearing the purple **toga** of an emperor, with a gold *clavus* (stripe) on his tunic. In fact, Christ was not even a Roman **citizen**, and would not have been entitled to wear a toga. As a Jewish man, he would have been bearded, though the mosaic shows him clean-shaven, like a late Roman. He has a circle of light around his head, called a halo, borrowed from images of the sun god, Sol Invictus. Within the halo, there is a cross, no longer thought of as a shameful image, but now the sacred symbol of the faith.

The end of Rome

By the time that Hagia Sophia was built, the old Roman Empire had broken up, as the West was overwhelmed by waves of invasions. Justinian ruled an Eastern empire, known as the Byzantine Empire. Although the Roman empire fell, the Church kept alive Roman traditions and converted the invaders to Christianity. Today, the pope (the bishop of Rome, and head of the Roman Catholic Church) still wears robes based on late Roman dress, and is called the Pontifex Maximus, the old title of Rome's chief priest.

▼ We do not know what Jesus Christ looked like, but he certainly did not resemble the clean-shaven Roman dressed in an imperial toga shown in this mosaic from a church in Ravenna, Italy.

Halo

Cross

Gold clavus

Purple toga

Timeline

753 B.C.E.
date of the foundation of Rome, according to legend

510 or 509 B.C.E.
last king expelled; Rome becomes a **republic**

270 B.C.E.
Rome dominates all Italy

264–241 B.C.E.
First Punic War (war with Carthage)

241 B.C.E.
Rome rules Sicily

218–201 B.C.E.
Second Punic War

197–146 B.C.E.
Romans conquer Greece

149–146 B.C.E.
Third Punic War; Carthage destroyed

88 B.C.E.
first **civil war**, between Sulla and Marius

58–49 B.C.E.
Caesar conquers Gaul (France) and leads two expeditions to Britain

c. 50 B.C.E.
glass-blowing invented in Syria

Carrara marble quarries opened in northern Italy

49–48 B.C.E.
civil war between Caesar and Pompey

44 B.C.E.
Caesar assassinated

33–31 B.C.E.
civil war between Octavian and Mark Antony

27 B.C.E.
Octavian, now called Augustus, becomes first Roman emperor

c. 30 c.e.
death of Jesus Christ

43 c.e.
Romans conquer Britain

79 c.e.
Vesuvius erupts, burying Pompeii and Herculaneum

80 c.e.
Colosseum opened in Rome

98–117 c.e.
reign of Trajan; **empire** reaches largest size

118–125 c.e.
building of the Pantheon

122 c.e.
Hadrian's wall begins to be built across Britain

216 c.e.
baths of Caracalla completed

306–337 c.e.
reign of Constantine, Rome's first Christian emperor

330 c.e.
Constantine founds new capital, Constantinople

392 c.e.
worship of old Roman gods banned

410 c.e.
Rome sacked by Visigoths (invading nomads)

476 c.e.
last western emperor overthrown

532–537c.e.
Justinian builds the church of Hagia Sophia

1453
Turks capture Constantinople

Glossary

ambitious having a strong desire to achieve something, such as fame or power

amphitheater oval or circular building with rising tiers of seats around an open space, called the arena. Amphitheaters were first built by the Romans for gladiators and wild beasts to fight in.

aqueduct raised, artificial channel for carrying water

archaeology study of past societies through their remains, such as buildings, tools, and other artifacts (objects made by people)

architecture style and way of building

barbarian term for a foreigner, used by both Greeks and Romans, originally because they thought that foreign languages sounded like meaningless "bar bar" noises

basilica hall used as a law court and for meetings

cast to form molten metal into a shape by pouring into a mold

citizen member of a state with full rights, such as the right to vote in elections

civil war war fought between people of the same country

Classical having to do with the ancient Greeks and Romans, especially their art, architecture, and literature

colonnade row of columns

consul one of two heads of state, elected each year, under the republic. The office continued under the emperors, but solely as an honor given to leading Romans.

crucible vessel used for melting materials at high temperatures

discipline under control; trained to obedience and order

divine godlike; superhumanly excellent, gifted, or beautiful

empire large area, including a number of countries, under the control of a single state

graffiti drawing or writing on a wall

magistrate government official

mass-produced made in large quantities

molten having become liquid by heating

mosaic picture made from tiny pieces of stone, pottery, marble, or glass, set in mortar. The name comes from "Muse," a goddess of the arts.

preservation keeping from decay; keeping safe

propaganda information spread in order to persuade

relief sculpture or pottery in which pictures stand out from their background. In sculpture, the background would be cut away. In pottery, a relief could be made using a mold.

republic state ruled by elected heads, rather than by a king or emperor

sacrifice offering made to a god, often an animal that was killed

Senate Roman government assembly made up of heads of leading families as well as ex-magistrates

standard pole with an image on top, such as a golden eagle or a silver hand, belonging to a legion or a smaller military unit. It was carried to lead soldiers into battle, and it was a symbol of Roman honor.

toga long piece of cloth worn by men. It was draped in complicated folds around the body.

Further Reading

Bardi, Pieri. *The Atlas of the Classical World*. New York: McGraw-Hill, 2001.

Barghusen, Joan. *Daily Life in Ancient and Modern Rome*. Minneapolis, Minn.: Lerner Publishing, 1999.

Chrisp, Peter. *The World of the Roman Emperor*. New York: McGraw-Hill, 1999.

Corbishley, Mike. *Ancient Rome*. New York: Facts on File, 2003.

Corbishley, Mike. *What Do We Know about the Romans?* New York: McGraw-Hill, 2001.

Hart, Avery, and Sandra Gallagher. *Ancient Rome!* Charlotte, Vt.: Williamson Publishing, 2001.

James, Simon. *Ancient Rome*. New York: Dorling Kindersley, 2000.

Jovinelly, Joann, and Jason Netelkos. *The Crafts and Culture of the Romans*. New York: Rosen Publishing, 2001.

Knight, Judson. *Ancient Civilizations*. Farmington Hills, Mich.: Gale Group, 2000.

Nardo, Don. *The Greenhaven Encyclopedia of Ancient Rome*. Farmington Hills, Mich.: Gale Group, 2002.

Nardo, Don. *Roman Roads and Aqueducts*. Farmington Hills, Mich.: Gale Group, 2001.

Uecker, Jeffry. *History Through Art Timeline*. Worcester, Mass.: Davis Publishers, 2001.

Woods, Mary B., and Michael Woods. *Ancient Construction*. Minneapolis, Minn.: Lerner Publishing, 2000.

Index